101 *Easy* ENTERTAINING
R E C I P E S

Gooseberry Patch
600 London Road
P.O. Box 190
Delaware, OH 43015

www.gooseberrypatch.com
1·800·854·6673

Copyright 2008, Gooseberry Patch 978-1-933494-67-8
Second Printing, June, 2009

Did you know?

Gooseberry Patch has everything you need to make your house a cozy home!

- our very own line of cookbooks, calendars & organizers
- charming kitchenware like mixing bowls, cake stands and enamelware
- delicious gourmet goodies

- farmhouse, cottage, retro and primitive styles
- soft-as-a-feather handmade quilts
- night lights for every season

**Call us toll-free at 1-800-854-6673, and we'd be delighted to send you our new catalog!
Or, shop with us online anytime at www.gooseberrypatch.com.**

Send us your favorite recipe

and the memory that makes it special for you!* If we select your recipe for a brand-new **Gooseberry Patch** cookbook, your name will appear right along with it...and you'll receive a FREE copy of the book! Submit your recipe on our website at **www.gooseberrypatch.com** or mail it to:

**Gooseberry Patch
Attn: Cookbook Dept.
P.O. Box 190
Delaware, OH 43015**

*Please include the number of servings and all other necessary information!

CONTENTS

Dedication

To everyone who agrees that yummy food makes
good times with family & friends even better!

Appreciation

A big thanks to all of our friends who shared
their tastiest (and easiest) recipes with us!

Two-Way Crostini

1 loaf French bread, thinly sliced
1/3 c. olive oil
2 cloves garlic, minced

Place bread on a baking sheet.
Microwave oil and garlic in a small bowl
for 30 seconds; brush over bread. Bake
at 425 degrees for 6 to 8 minutes, until
golden. Makes 2 dozen servings.

Tomato-Basil Topping:

7 to 8 roma tomatoes, chopped
10 fresh basil leaves, minced
1 clove garlic, minced
1/4 c. olive oil
salt and pepper to taste

Mix ingredients well. Let stand at room
temperature for 30 minutes.

Cannellini-Rosemary Topping:

4 cloves garlic, minced
1/2 c. olive oil
2 19-oz. cans cannellini beans,
    drained and rinsed
3/4 c. water
juice of 1/2 lemon
1 T. fresh rosemary, chopped
salt and pepper to taste

Sauté garlic in oil. Add beans and water;
bring to a boil. Reduce heat; simmer for
20 minutes. Mash beans until chunky;
add juice and seasonings. Serve warm.

Stacie Mickley
Gooseberry Patch

Offer guests one or
both of these savory
garden-fresh toppings.

Cucumber Bites

2 cucumbers
5.2-oz. container cream cheese
   spread with garlic & herbs
Garnish: thinly sliced smoked
   salmon, minced hard-boiled
   egg yolk, snipped fresh dill

Remove thin strips of peel from
cucumbers with a potato peeler; slice
1/2-inch thick. Top each slice with
one teaspoon cheese spread; garnish
as desired. May be covered and chilled
up to 3 hours before serving time.
Makes 2 to 3 dozen.

Jenni Shoaf
Woodland Hills, CA
For a fancy finish in a
snap, spoon cheese spread
into a pastry bag fitted
with a large star tip.
Swirl onto cucumber rounds.

Working Moms' Cheese Ball

2 8-oz. containers flavored
   spreadable cream cheese
1/2 to 1 c. mixed shredded cheese
Optional: hot pepper sauce
   to taste
1/2 to 3/4 c. finely chopped
   pecans
Garnish: whole pecans
assorted crackers and cut-up
   vegetables

Blend cream cheese and shredded
cheese in a medium bowl; add
pepper sauce, if desired. Form into
a ball and roll in chopped pecans.
Wrap in plastic wrap; refrigerate for
one hour before serving. Garnish
with whole pecans; surround with
crackers and vegetables to serve.
Makes 3 to 4 cups.

9

Vickie Garlitz
Edmond, OK

This is easy, quick and
tastes great! Use whatever
flavor of cream cheese you
have in the fridge...dill,
garlic, onion & chive
are all tasty.

Spicy Garlic Almonds

2 T. soy sauce
2 t. hot pepper sauce
3 cloves garlic, pressed
1 lb. blanched whole almonds
1 T. butter, melted
1 T. seasoned salt
1 T. pepper
1/4 t. red pepper flakes

Combine sauces and garlic in a medium bowl. Add almonds, stirring until well coated. Brush butter over a 15"x10" jelly-roll pan. Spread almonds on pan in a single layer. Bake at 350 degrees for 10 minutes. Sprinkle salt and peppers over almonds; return to oven for 15 minutes. Remove from oven; cool on pan. Store in an airtight container. Makes about 3 cups.

Cathy Siebrecht
Des Moines, IA

So quick, so easy, so tasty! For a gift any hostess will welcome, fill a Mason jar with these snackable nuts.

Gazpacho Dip

3 tomatoes, diced
3 avocados, pitted and diced
4 green onions, thinly sliced
4-oz. can diced green chiles
3 T. olive oil
1-1/2 T. cider vinegar
1 t. garlic salt
1 t. salt
1/4 t. pepper
tortilla chips

Combine tomatoes, avocados, onions and chiles in a large bowl; set aside. Combine remaining ingredients except tortilla chips; drizzle over tomato mixture and toss gently. Cover and chill. Serve with tortilla chips. Makes about 6 cups.

11

Vickie
If you like salsa, you'll love this zesty dip. Serve with lime-flavored white corn tortilla chips... wonderful!

Seeded Tortilla Crisps

1/4 c. butter, melted
8 10-inch flour tortillas
3/4 c. grated Parmesan cheese
1 egg white, beaten
Garnish: sesame, poppy and/or
    caraway seed
onion powder, cayenne pepper
    or dried cumin to taste

Brush butter lightly over one side
of each tortilla; sprinkle evenly
with cheese and press down lightly.
Carefully turn tortillas over. Brush
other side with egg white and
sprinkle with desired seeds and
seasoning. Cut each tortilla into
4 strips with a pastry cutter or knife.
Place strips cheese-side down on a
baking sheet sprayed with non-stick
vegetable spray. Bake at 400 degrees,
on middle rack of oven, for 8 to
10 minutes, until crisp and golden.
Cool on a wire rack. Makes about
2-1/2 dozen.

Jewel Grindley
Lindenhurst, IL

Bake up these spicy strips
in a jiffy! They're a
pleasing change from
ordinary chips...serve with
spreads, salads and soups.

Bacon-Horseradish Dip

3 8-oz. pkgs. cream cheese, softened
12-oz. pkg. shredded Cheddar cheese
1 c. half-and-half
1/3 c. green onion, chopped
3 cloves garlic, minced
3 T. prepared horseradish
1 T. Worcestershire sauce
1/2 t. pepper
12 slices bacon, crisply cooked and crumbled
bagel chips or assorted crackers

Combine all ingredients except bacon and chips or crackers in a slow cooker. Cover and cook on low setting for 4 to 5 hours, or on high setting for 2 to 2-1/2 hours, stirring once halfway through. Just before serving, stir in bacon. Serve with bagel chips or crackers. Makes 7 to 8 cups.

13

Kathy Grashoff
Fort Wayne, IN

Put a slow cooker to work cooking up this creamy, cheesy dip...it's out of this world!

Cream Cheese Terrine

4 8-oz. pkgs. cream cheese,
  softened and divided
2 cloves garlic, chopped
Optional: 2 t. herbes de Provence
1/8 t. dried basil
7-oz. pkg. sun-dried tomatoes,
  sliced
3 T. green onion, sliced
1/8 t. dried parsley
4-oz. pkg. crumbled blue cheese
1/2 c. sliced almonds
7-oz. jar basil pesto sauce
assorted snack crackers

Blend one package cream cheese with garlic and herbes de Provence, if using; spread into a plastic wrap-lined 8"x4" loaf pan. Sprinkle with basil; chill for 15 minutes. Mix second package cream cheese with tomatoes and onion; spread over first layer. Sprinkle with parsley; chill for 15 minutes. Blend third package cream cheese with blue cheese and almonds; spread over tomato layer. Chill for 15 minutes. Combine remaining package cream cheese with pesto; spread over blue cheese layer. Cover and chill for at least one hour. To serve, gently pull up on plastic wrap; invert onto a serving platter and peel away plastic wrap. Serve with crackers. Serves 12.

Amy Palsrock
Silverdale, WA
My family & friends all call this my twenty-dollar dip...it looks (and tastes!) like it's from a gourmet store.

Roquefort Cut-Out Crackers

1 c. all-purpose flour
7 T. crumbled Roquefort or
    blue cheese
1 egg yolk
4 t. whipping cream
7 T. butter, softened
1/8 t. salt
cayenne pepper to taste
1/2 t. dried parsley

Stir together all ingredients in a large
bowl until dough forms. Cover; let
stand for 30 minutes. On a floured
surface, roll out dough to 1/8-inch
thickness. Cut out dough with a
round cookie cutter or other desired
shape; arrange on an ungreased
baking sheet. Bake at 400 degrees
for 7 to 9 minutes, just until golden.
Let cool on baking sheet; store in an
airtight container. Makes 2 dozen.

15

Linda Henderson
Sunset, NC
I like to choose cookie
cutters in shapes to
match the occasion.

Munch & Crunch Mix

1 c. mini pretzels
1 c. corn chips
1 c. oyster crackers
1 c. toasted pumpkin seeds
1 c. honey-roasted peanuts
2 T. margarine, melted
2 T. brown sugar, packed
1 t. Worcestershire sauce
1 t. chili powder
1/2 t. onion salt
1/2 t. ground cumin
1/8 t. cayenne pepper

Combine pretzels, chips, crackers, seeds and nuts in a large bowl; toss to mix. Whisk together remaining ingredients; pour over mixture in bowl, stirring to coat. Spread mix in an ungreased roasting pan. Bake at 300 degrees for 25 minutes, stirring after 12 minutes. Cool completely; store in an airtight container. Makes about 5 cups.

Emily Oravecz
Weehawken, NJ

A crunchy snack mix with a kick of chili and cayenne! Tie little sacks of this spicy mix in bandannas for a game-day treat.

Sugared Walnuts

1 lb. walnut halves
1/2 c. butter, melted
1/2 c. powdered sugar
1-1/2 t. cinnamon
1/4 t. ground cloves
1/4 t. ground ginger

Preheat a slow cooker on high setting for 15 minutes. Add nuts and butter, stirring to mix well. Add powdered sugar; mix until coated evenly. Cover and cook on high setting for 15 minutes. Reduce heat to low setting. Cook, uncovered, stirring occasionally, for 2 to 3 hours, or until nuts are coated with a crisp glaze. Transfer nuts to a serving bowl. Combine spices in a small bowl and sprinkle over nuts, stirring to coat evenly. Cool before serving. Store in an airtight container. Makes about 4 cups.

17

Connie Fortune
Covington, OH
A fix & forget version of this holiday favorite.

Garlic Dip

2 8-oz. pkgs. cream cheese,
    softened
2 T. dill weed
1/2 t. salt
1/2 t. pepper
1 t. dried, minced onion
1/4 onion, chopped
2 to 4 cloves garlic, minced
1 carrot, peeled and finely chopped
1 stalk celery, finely chopped
Optional: paprika
assorted vegetables such as
    carrot sticks, celery stalks,
    snow peas, red pepper slices,
    green onions

Combine cream cheese, seasonings
and chopped vegetables, blending well.
Sprinkle with paprika, if desired;
cover and chill. Let stand at room
temperature for one hour before
serving. Serve with fresh vegetables
for dipping. Makes about 2 cups.

Julianne Carlson
Mount Vernon, OH

When you serve this cool,
creamy dip, be sure to have
plenty of copies of the
recipe...everyone will
want one!

Cheese Straws

16-oz. pkg. shredded sharp
   Cheddar cheese, at room
   temperature
1-1/4 c. margarine, softened
3 c. all-purpose flour
1 t. cayenne pepper
1 t. salt

Combine all ingredients together in a
large bowl. Mix well, using your hands.
Spoon dough into a cookie press with
a star tip. Press dough in strips onto
ungreased baking sheets; cut strips
3 inches long. Bake at 350 degrees
for 12 to 15 minutes, or until orange
on bottom and around edges. Cool
on wire racks; store in an airtight
container. Makes 3 to 4 dozen.

Cindy McKinnon
El Dorado, AR

My Aunt Sister's famous
signature recipe. She
passed away several years
ago, yet she is still
remembered as being an
awesome cook.

19

Salmon Party Log

16-oz. can salmon, drained
  and flaked
8-oz. pkg. cream cheese, softened
1 T. lemon juice
1 t. prepared horseradish
2 t. onion, grated
1/4 t. salt
1/4 t. Worcestershire sauce
1/2 c. chopped pecans
3 T. fresh parsley, chopped
water crackers

Place all ingredients except pecans, parsley and crackers in a medium bowl. Mix thoroughly; shape into a log. Place pecans and parsley on wax paper; roll log in mixture until coated. Cover and chill at least 2 hours. Serve with crackers. Makes about 3 cups.

Paula Braswell
Marietta, GA

This recipe can be made a day in advance and tucked into the fridge...so handy when you're planning a party!

Reuben Dip ✓

16-oz. jar sauerkraut, drained
1/2 lb. deli-style corned beef,
　shredded
8-oz. pkg. cream cheese,
　softened
8-oz. pkg. shredded Swiss cheese
1/4 c. Thousand Island salad
　dressing

Combine all ingredients in a slow
cooker. Cover and cook on high
setting for 45 minutes, stirring
occasionally, just until heated
through and cheese is melted.
Makes 6 to 7 cups.

21

Jen Burnham
Delaware, OH

Add a basket of party rye
slices or pumpernickel
rye pretzels...I guarantee
it'll be a hit at your
next tailgating party!

Antipasto Kabobs

1/3 c. olive oil
1/3 c. balsamic vinegar
1 T. fresh thyme, minced
1 clove garlic, minced
1 t. sugar
9-oz. pkg. cheese-filled tortellini,
    cooked
5-oz. pkg. thinly sliced salami
12-oz. jar artichoke hearts,
    drained and quartered
5-3/4 oz. jar green olives with
    pimentos, drained
16-oz. jar banana peppers, drained
1 pt. cherry tomatoes
16 6-inch skewers, soaked in water

Combine oil, vinegar, thyme, garlic
and sugar; set aside. Thread remaining
ingredients onto skewers alternately
in order given. Arrange skewers in
a single layer in a glass or plastic
container; drizzle with marinade.
Cover and refrigerate for 2 to 3 hours,
turning occasionally. Drain and
discard marinade before serving.
Makes 16 servings.

Kenny Phillips
Jacksonville, FL

Easy-to-pick-up party food!
Add some crunchy bread
sticks for a light
warm-weather meal.

Confetti Cheesecake

Suzanne Varnes
Palatka, FL

A recipe I have made many times...my guests always enjoy it! Serve it with crisp crackers, or slice thinly and serve with a green salad for a light lunch.

1-1/2 c. round buttery cracker crumbs
1/2 c. butter, melted
2 8-oz. pkgs. cream cheese, softened
2 eggs
1/3 c. all-purpose flour
8-oz. container sour cream
1-1/2 c. green pepper, finely chopped
3/4 c. carrot, peeled and shredded
1/4 c. onion, finely chopped
1/4 t. salt
1/4 t. white pepper
assorted crackers

23

Combine cracker crumbs and butter; press into an ungreased 9" or 10" springform pan. Bake at 300 degrees for 10 minutes; remove from oven. In a large bowl, beat cream cheese until fluffy; add eggs, one at a time. Stir in flour, mixing well. Add remaining ingredients except crackers, folding vegetables well into batter. Pour into baked crust; bake at 300 degrees for one hour. Turn oven off; cool in oven for one hour before refrigerating. At serving time, remove outer ring of springform pan. Serve with crackers. Makes 10 to 12 servings.

Pizza Bread Twists ✓

Jane Gates
Saginaw, MI
Refrigerated pizza dough
lets you twist up these
tasty sticks in a jiffy!

2 10-oz. tubes refrigerated pizza
    dough
1/2 c. sun-dried tomatoes in oil,
    drained and finely chopped
4 t. olive oil
4 t. water
1/2 c. grated Parmesan cheese
3/4 t. dried oregano
1/4 t. pepper

Unroll one tube dough on a lightly
floured surface; pat or roll into a
10-inch by 8-inch rectangle. Whisk
together remaining ingredients.
Spread half of mixture over dough;
fold dough in half crosswise. Slice
dough lengthwise into ten, 1/2-inch
wide strips. Twist each strip 2 to
3 times; place on a lightly greased
baking sheet. Repeat with remaining
dough and tomato mixture. Bake at
350 degrees for 12 to 15 minutes,
until golden. Cool on a wire rack.
Makes 20 bread sticks.

Cheddar Fondue ✓

1/4 c. butter
1/4 c. all-purpose flour
1/2 t. salt
1/4 t. pepper
1/4 t. Worcestershire sauce
1/4 t. dry mustard
1-1/2 c. milk
8-oz. pkg. shredded Cheddar
   cheese
1 loaf French bread, cubed

Melt butter in a saucepan over medium heat. Whisk in flour, salt, pepper, Worcestershire sauce and mustard until smooth. Gradually add milk; boil for 2 minutes or until thickened, whisking constantly. Reduce heat; add cheese, stirring until melted. Transfer to a fondue pot or mini slow cooker and keep warm. Serve with bread cubes for dipping. Makes 2-1/2 cups.

25

Lori Steen
Aloha, OR

Try cubes of crusty Italian bread, sourdough or even tiny boiled new potatoes with this dreamy fondue.

Mom's Tasty Kielbasa

1 c. onion, sliced
1 c. celery, chopped
1 to 2 T. butter
1/2 c. catsup
1 t. Worcestershire sauce
1/4 c. vinegar
1/4 c. sugar
1 T. mustard
1 t. paprika
1 lb. Kielbasa, sliced into
   1-inch pieces

In a skillet over medium heat, sauté onion and celery in butter until tender. Add remaining ingredients except Kielbasa. Mix well; add Kielbasa and bring to a boil. Reduce heat; simmer until sauce thickens, stirring often. Makes 8 to 10 servings.

Jackie McBride
Barnesville, OH

My mom made this for my wedding reception...she's had the recipe so long that her copy is faded. It has a sweet-and-sour taste that's so delicious!

Special Deviled Eggs

1 doz. eggs, hard-boiled and
   peeled
3 to 4 T. coleslaw dressing
1/8 to 1/4 t. garlic salt with
   parsley
Garnish: paprika, snipped
   fresh chives

Slice eggs in half lengthwise; scoop
yolks into a bowl. Arrange whites
on a serving platter; set aside.
Mash yolks well with a fork. Stir
in dressing to desired consistency
and add garlic salt to taste. Spoon
or pipe yolk mixture into whites.
Garnish as desired; chill. Makes
2 dozen.

27

Regina Kostyu
Gooseberry Patch

A "must" at any picnic or
potluck...these deviled
eggs are even better
than usual!

Crab-Stuffed Mushrooms

15 mushrooms
7-oz. can crabmeat, drained
  and flaked
1 slice bread, torn
1 egg, beaten
1/3 c. onion, chopped
1/2 t. seafood seasoning
salt and pepper to taste
4 to 5 T. grated Parmesan cheese
2 T. butter, melted

Remove and chop mushroom stems, setting aside mushroom caps. Combine chopped stems with crabmeat, bread, egg, onion and seasonings; mix well. Spoon mixture into mushroom caps; sprinkle with cheese and set aside. Brush melted butter over a 13"x9" baking pan; arrange mushroom caps in pan. Broil for 2 to 4 minutes, until golden and heated through. Makes 15.

Cindy Skinner
Hagerstown, MD

Friends will think you spent the whole day in the kitchen...only you will know how easy this recipe is!

Chinese Spareribs

6 lbs. pork spareribs, sliced into
   serving-size portions
1/4 c. hoisin sauce
1/4 c. water
3 T. dry sherry
2 T. honey
2 T. soy sauce
2 cloves garlic, minced

Place ribs in a very large plastic
zipping bag. Mix remaining
ingredients in a small bowl; pour
over ribs. Seal bag; turn gently to
coat ribs with marinade. Refrigerate
for 6 hours to overnight, turning
bag several times. Drain; reserve
and refrigerate marinade. Place ribs
in a lightly greased shallow roasting
pan. Cover with aluminum foil.
Bake at 350 degrees for 1-1/2 hours.
Uncover; brush reserved marinade
over ribs, discarding any remaining
marinade. Bake, uncovered, an
additional 30 minutes, or until
tender. Makes 6 servings as a main
dish or 12 to 15 appetizer servings.

29

Melissa Bordenkircher
Gooseberry Patch

Set out a basket of
fingertip towels with
these flavorful ribs!
Dampen towels with water
and lemon juice, roll up
and microwave until warm.

3-Cheese Artichoke Bites

Della Jones
Georgetown, KY

Mini appetizers filled with Cheddar, Parmesan and mozzarella cheese... scrumptious!

1 onion, chopped
1 clove garlic, minced
1 T. oil
2 6-1/2 oz. jars marinated
   artichokes, drained and
   chopped
6 eggs, beaten
1 c. shredded Cheddar cheese
1 c. shredded mozzarella cheese
1 c. grated Parmesan cheese
1/2 t. Italian seasoning
1/4 c. fresh parsley, chopped
1/4 t. pepper
1/8 t. Worcestershire sauce
1/8 t. hot pepper sauce
1/4 c. Italian-seasoned dry
   bread crumbs
Optional: additional fresh
   parsley, chopped

In a skillet over medium heat, sauté onion and garlic in oil until tender; drain and set aside. Combine artichokes, eggs, cheeses, seasonings and sauces in a large bowl; mix well. Stir in onion mixture and bread crumbs. Fill greased mini muffin cups 2/3 full. Bake at 325 degrees for 15 to 20 minutes, until firm and golden. Serve warm, sprinkled with additional parsley, if desired. Makes 3-1/2 to 4 dozen.

Mushroom Turnovers

8-oz. pkg. cream cheese,
  softened
1 c. plus 2 T. margarine, divided
2 c. plus 2 T. all-purpose flour,
  divided
4 c. sliced mushrooms, chopped
2/3 c. green onions, chopped
1/3 c. sour cream
2 T. all-purpose flour
1/4 t. dried thyme
1/4 t. salt
1 egg white, beaten
Garnish: sesame seed

31

Blend cream cheese, one cup margarine and 2 cups flour; chill. In a skillet, sauté mushrooms and onions in remaining margarine for 3 minutes. Add sour cream, remaining flour, thyme and salt. Cook for several more minutes, stirring occasionally. Divide chilled dough in half; roll out 1/8-inch thick and cut with a 2-1/2" round cutter. Place a heaping 1/4 teaspoon mushroom mixture in center of each circle. Fold over; press edges gently with fingers to seal. Use a spatula to transfer turnovers to a lightly greased baking sheet; press edges with a fork. Brush turnovers with egg white; sprinkle with sesame seed. Bake at 350 degrees for 20 minutes. Makes 5 dozen.

Judy Borecky
Escondido, CA
A super make-ahead recipe!
Freeze unbaked turnovers on
baking sheets, then store
in freezer bags. At serving
time, bake as directed.

Toasted Ravioli ✓

2 T. milk
1 egg
3/4 c. Italian-seasoned dry
   bread crumbs
1/2 t. salt
24 frozen meat or cheese-filled
   ravioli, thawed
oil for deep frying
1 T. grated Parmesan cheese
Garnish: marinara sauce, warmed

Whisk milk and egg together in a small bowl. Place bread crumbs and salt in a separate small bowl. Dip ravioli into milk mixture; roll in crumbs to coat. Pour 2 inches of oil into a large heavy saucepan. Heat oil to 375 degrees, until a cube of bread sizzles and turns brown. Add ravioli a few at a time, frying for one minute on each side, or until golden. Drain on paper towels; sprinkle with Parmesan cheese. Serve warm with sauce for dipping. Makes 2 dozen.

Brenda Smith
Gooseberry Patch

Such fun to eat! Choose either cheese or meat-filled ravioli...it's up to you!

Italian Egg Rolls

1/2 c. onion, chopped
1/2 c. green pepper, chopped
2 t. oil
1 lb. ground sweet or hot Italian
    pork sausage
2 10-oz. pkgs. frozen spinach,
    thawed and drained
1/2 c. grated Parmesan cheese
3 c. shredded mozzarella cheese
1/2 t. garlic powder
14-oz. pkg. egg roll wrappers
olive oil for deep frying
Garnish: pizza sauce, warmed

33

In a skillet over medium heat,
sauté onion and green pepper in
oil. Remove to a medium bowl and
set aside. Brown sausage in skillet;
drain and combine with onion
mixture. Add spinach, cheeses and
garlic powder; mix well. Top each
egg roll wrapper with 3 tablespoons
of mixture; roll up, following
directions on egg roll package.
Heat 3 to 4 inches oil in a deep
fryer. Add egg rolls a few at a time,
frying until golden. Drain on paper
towels. Serve warm with pizza sauce
for dipping. Makes 8.

Carolyn Scilanbro
Hampton, VA
Everyone loves egg rolls!
These are stuffed with
sausage and spinach for an
unexpected treat. Yummy!

Smokey Vegetable Pizzas

Melissa Beck
Springfield, IL
Try thinly sliced small squash or eggplant too... yummy! They can be baked along with the onion.

1 red onion, thinly sliced
  into wedges
6-oz. jar marinated artichoke
  hearts, drained, quartered and
  marinade reserved
1 loaf frozen bread dough, thawed
2 c. smoked Gouda cheese,
  shredded and divided
3 roma tomatoes, sliced
4 green onions, thinly sliced
2 t. Italian seasoning
1 T. fresh basil, snipped

Place onion wedges on a lightly greased baking sheet. Brush with reserved marinade. Bake at 425 degrees for 10 minutes; remove from oven. Divide thawed dough into 12 balls. On a lightly floured surface, flatten each ball to a 4-inch circle. Place dough circles on lightly greased baking sheets; pierce with a fork. Sprinkle one cup cheese evenly over dough circles. Top each with an onion wedge, an artichoke quarter and a tomato slice. Sprinkle with sliced onion, seasoning and remaining cheese. Bake at 425 degrees for about 10 minutes, until edges are lightly golden. Remove from oven; sprinkle with basil. Makes 12 servings.

Cheesy Potato Puffs ✓

4-oz. pkg. instant potato flakes
1/2 c. shredded Cheddar cheese
1/2 c. bacon bits
Optional: paprika

Prepare potato flakes according to package directions; let cool. Stir in cheese; roll into 1-1/2 inch balls. Roll balls in bacon bits; arrange on an ungreased baking sheet. Sprinkle with paprika, if desired. Bake at 375 degrees for 15 to 18 minutes. Serves 4.

35

Barb Sulser
Gooseberry Patch

We can't stop nibbling on these golden morsels!

Fried Dill Pickles

3 eggs
1 c. milk
1 c. Italian-seasoned dry bread
  crumbs
1/4 c. all-purpose flour
15 dill pickle spears, well drained
oil for deep frying
Garnish: ranch or Thousand
  Island salad dressing

Whisk together eggs and milk in a small bowl; mix bread crumbs and flour in a separate small bowl. Dip pickles into egg mixture; roll in crumb mixture to coat. Heat several inches oil to 375 degrees in a deep fryer. Fry pickles 3 to 5 at a time until golden. Drain on paper towels. Serve warm with salad dressing for dipping. Makes 4 to 5 servings.

Tina George
El Dorado, AR

One of our favorite county fair foods! If you've never tried one, what are you waiting for?

Mini Wonton Salsa Baskets

24 wonton wrappers
15-1/4 oz. can corn, drained
16-oz. can black beans, drained
and rinsed
16-oz. can kidney beans, drained
and rinsed
8-oz. jar mild or spicy salsa
1 c. shredded Cheddar cheese

Spray 24 mini muffin cups with
non-stick vegetable spray; gently
press a wonton wrapper into each.
Bake at 350 degrees for 10 minutes,
until crisp. Mix together corn,
beans and salsa; spoon into shells.
Top with cheese. Makes 2 dozen.

37

Jo Ann
These crisp little shells
are really versatile! Try
filling them with cheesy
spinach & artichoke
spread too.

Ham-Wrapped Asparagus Spears

24 thin asparagus spears, trimmed
1 lb. provolone cheese, thinly
    sliced
1/2 lb. deli honey ham, very thinly
    sliced and slices cut in half
1/2 c. olive oil
1/2 c. balsamic vinegar
pepper to taste

In a skillet, bring one inch water to a
boil over medium heat. Add asparagus;
cover and cook for 3 to 4 minutes,
just until crisp-tender. Drain and chill
asparagus. Wrap a cheese slice tightly
around each spear; wrap each with a
half-slice of ham. Place spears in a
shallow dish, seam-side down. Whisk
together oil, vinegar and pepper; drizzle
over spears. Cover and refrigerate for
2 to 8 hours. Makes 2 dozen.

Renee Barton
La Porte, IN

A tempting way to enjoy the
first tender asparagus in
springtime...easy to make
ahead too!

Mac & Cheese Nuggets ✓

1/4 c. grated Parmesan cheese, divided
1-1/2 T. butter
2 T. all-purpose flour
3/4 c. milk
1-1/4 c. shredded Cheddar cheese
1/4 lb. American cheese slices, chopped
1 egg yolk, beaten
1/4 t. paprika
8-oz. pkg. elbow macaroni, cooked

Lightly grease mini muffin cups. Sprinkle with 2 tablespoons Parmesan cheese, tapping out excess. Melt butter in a large saucepan over medium heat. Stir in flour; cook for 2 minutes. Whisk in milk until boiling, about 5 minutes. Add Cheddar and American cheeses; remove from heat and stir until smooth. Whisk in egg yolk and paprika; fold in macaroni until well coated. Spoon rounded tablespoons of mixture into prepared tins; sprinkle with remaining Parmesan. Bake at 425 degrees until hot and golden, about 10 minutes. Cool for 5 minutes; carefully transfer to a serving plate. Makes 4 dozen.

39

Liz Plotnick-Snay
Gooseberry Patch

Little kids really go for these cheesy tidbits... big kids do too!

Spiedini

1 loaf French bread, sliced
   1/4-inch thick
2 T. butter, softened
1/4 lb. provolone cheese, sliced
   1/4-inch thick and quartered
16 4-inch sprigs fresh rosemary

Lightly spread 12 slices bread with
butter on both sides. Form stacked
sandwiches, alternating 3 bread slices
with 2 cheese slices. Cut sandwiches
into quarters with a serrated knife.
Remove leaves from one end of each
rosemary sprig; push this end through
a quartered sandwich to secure. Repeat
with remaining bread, cheese and
rosemary sprigs. Arrange on an
ungreased aluminum foil-lined baking
sheet. Bake at 425 degrees for 4 to
5 minutes, until golden and cheese
melts. Serve warm. Makes 16 servings.

Michelle Hill
Suwanee, GA
The fresh rosemary really
flavors these little
sandwiches of grilled
cheese...heavenly!

Teriyaki Chicken Skewers ✓

1/4 c. soy sauce
1/4 c. brown sugar, packed
2 t. apricot jam
1/2 t. ground ginger
2 cloves garlic, pressed
2 boneless, skinless chicken
   breasts, cut into 1-inch cubes
8 green onions, cut into 1-inch
   lengths
4 to 6 8-inch skewers, soaked
   in water

Whisk together soy sauce, brown sugar, jam, ginger and garlic in a shallow bowl. Add chicken to sauce; toss to coat. Cover and refrigerate for one to 8 hours, stirring occasionally. Alternate chicken and onions on skewers, reserving marinade. Broil for 10 minutes, or until chicken is cooked through, turning several times and basting with reserved marinade. Discard any remaining marinade. Makes 4 to 6 servings.

41

Christine Gabriel
Hay Market, VA

Juicy cubes of fresh pineapple would be a delightful addition to these flavorful skewers.

Marinated Olives

2 6-oz. cans whole black olives,
   drained
1/2 c. olive oil
1/4 c. fresh oregano or basil,
   chopped
4 cloves garlic, minced
2 T. balsamic vinegar
1 t. red pepper flakes
1/2 t. salt

Combine all ingredients; mix well
and place in a covered container.
Refrigerate for 2 hours before serving.
May be kept refrigerated up to one
month. Makes about 2 cups.

Pat Geno
Everett, WA
My kids' favorite olive
recipe...they request it
at all holidays. You'll
love it too!

Greek Pizza

13.8-oz. tube refrigerated
  pizza dough
1 to 2 T. olive oil
2 cloves garlic, minced
8-oz. pkg. shredded mozzarella
  cheese, divided
1/2 c. canned artichokes,
  drained and chopped
1/4 c. sliced green olives
3 T. capers
1/2 c. fresh basil, thinly sliced
1/4 c. crumbled feta cheese
Optional: 6 anchovy fillets,
  finely chopped

Roll out dough on a floured surface
to about 1/4-inch thick. Place on a
lightly greased baking sheet; brush
lightly with oil. Spread garlic over
dough; sprinkle with half the
mozzarella cheese. Top with
artichokes, olives, capers, basil,
feta cheese and anchovies, if using.
Sprinkle with remaining mozzarella.
Bake at 400 degrees for 8 to
10 minutes, or until cheese melts.
Serves 4.

Sean Avner
Delaware, OH
Don't let the anchovies
keep you from trying
this pizza...they are
flavorful but optional!

43

Smokey Sausage Wraps

16-oz. pkg. cheese-filled
  cocktail sausages
3 T. barbecue sauce
1 T. maple syrup
8-oz. tube refrigerated
  crescent rolls
Garnish: additional barbecue
  sauce

Place 32 sausages in a medium
saucepan; reserve any remaining
sausages for another recipe. Stir in
barbecue sauce and maple syrup.
Cook over medium heat until heated
through; let cool for 5 to 10 minutes.
Separate crescents into triangles;
cut each triangle into 4 long, thin
triangles. Wrap one triangle of dough
around each sausage; pinch ends to
seal. Arrange on an ungreased baking
sheet. Bake at 350 degrees until golden.
Serve with additional sauce for
dipping. Makes 32 wraps.

Vickie McMonigal
Altoona, PA

Party-perfect mini
Pigs in a Blanket! Serve
with spicy brown mustard
for dipping too.

Crabmeat Pastry Shells

6-oz. can crabmeat, drained
  and flaked
2 T. cream cheese, softened
1/4 to 1/2 c. mayonnaise
3 T. green onion, chopped
1 t. Worcestershire sauce
1 t. lemon juice
10-oz. pkg. frozen puff pastry
  shells
Optional: additional green
  onion, chopped

Mix together crabmeat, cream cheese, mayonnaise, onion, sauce and juice; refrigerate overnight. Bake pastry shells according to package directions; cool. At serving time, spoon crabmeat mixture into shells. Sprinkle with additional green onion, if desired. Makes 6 servings.

45

Linda Scott-Hoag
Janesville, WI

These delightful seafood-filled shells only look difficult...with frozen puff pastry shells, they go together in a jiffy!

Shrimp-Stuffed Tomato Poppers

2 pts. cherry tomatoes
1/2 lb. cooked shrimp, peeled and
   finely chopped
8-oz. pkg. cream cheese, softened
1/4 c. mayonnaise
1/4 c. grated Parmesan cheese
2 t. prepared horseradish
1 t. lemon juice
salt and pepper to taste
Garnish: chopped fresh parsley

Cut a thin slice off the top of each
tomato; scoop out and discard pulp.
Place tomatoes upside-down on a
paper towel; let drain for 30 minutes.
Combine remaining ingredients except
parsley; blend until smooth. Spoon
into tomatoes; sprinkle with parsley.
Makes about 16 servings.

Kristin Zurek
Berkeley, CA
Fresh cherry tomatoes with
a creamy shrimp filling. For
variety, substitute crispy
bacon for the shrimp.

Garden Patch Grilled Vegetables

6 small onions, sliced
   into wedges
4 to 5 thin carrots, peeled
4 potatoes, sliced into wedges
1 red pepper, sliced into strips
1 green pepper, sliced into strips
1 to 2 zucchini, sliced lengthwise
1/4 lb. mushrooms
1/2 c. olive oil
1/4 c. fresh thyme, chopped
salt and pepper to taste

Cover onions, carrots and potatoes
with water in a large saucepan.
Simmer over medium-high heat
until crisp-tender, about 15 to
20 minutes. Drain; cool slightly.
Combine cooked and uncooked
vegetables in a large bowl. Whisk
together oil and thyme; drizzle half
of mixture over vegetables. Arrange
vegetables on a lightly oiled grill over
medium-high heat. Grill until
tender, turning often and brushing
with remaining oil mixture. Sprinkle
with salt and pepper to taste; serve
warm. Makes about 6 to 8 servings.

47

Jo Ann
Savor the bounty of a
nearby farmers' market!
All kinds of fresh veggies
are irresistible prepared
this way.

Asian Chicken Wings

4 lbs. chicken wings
1/4 c. olive oil
2-1/2 t. salt, divided
2 t. pepper, divided
1/2 c. honey
2 T. soy sauce
1 t. Worcestershire sauce
juice of 1 lime
zest of 2 limes
2 cloves garlic, finely minced
1 T. fresh cilantro, chopped
2 t. red pepper flakes

Place wings on an aluminum foil-lined 15"x10" jelly-roll pan. Drizzle wings with oil and toss to coat; sprinkle with 1-1/2 teaspoons salt and one teaspoon pepper. Bake at 400 degrees for 50 minutes; do not turn. Remove from oven. Using tongs, carefully lift wings from foil. Stir together remaining salt, pepper and other ingredients. Drizzle 1/3 cup of sauce mixture over hot wings and toss to coat. Serve remainder separately for dipping. Makes 2-1/2 to 3 dozen.

Jordan Ray
Clermont, FL
Honey, lime and garlic blend to create a zesty alternative to barbecue-style chicken wings.

Brie Kisses

2/3 lb. Brie cheese, cut into
   1/2-inch cubes
17.3-oz. pkg. frozen puff pastry
1/3 c. red or green hot
   pepper jelly

Arrange cheese cubes on a plate and place in the freezer. Let pastry thaw at room temperature for 30 minutes. Unfold each sheet of pastry and roll with a rolling pin to remove creases. Slice each sheet into quarters; slice each quarter in half. Slice each piece in half one more time for a total of 32 squares. Place squares into greased mini muffin cups; arrange so corners of dough point upwards. Bake at 400 degrees for 5 minutes. Place one cheese cube in center of each pastry. Bake an additional 10 minutes, until edges are golden. Remove pastries from tin; immediately top each with 1/2 teaspoon jelly. Serve warm. Makes 2-1/2 dozen.

49

Kathy Grashoff
Fort Wayne, IN
Delicate cheesy bites that you'll love serving at holiday parties.

Chili Sweet Potato Fries ✓

3-1/2 lbs. sweet potatoes, sliced
   into 1-inch wedges
2 T. olive oil
3/4 t. salt
1/4 t. pepper
1/2 c. orange juice
1 T. honey
3-1/2 t. chili powder, divided
1/3 c. fresh cilantro, chopped
8-oz. container sour cream

Place potato wedges in a large plastic zipping bag; sprinkle with oil, salt and pepper. Toss to mix. Arrange potato wedges on lightly greased baking sheets. Stir together orange juice, honey and 3 teaspoons chili powder; set aside. Bake, uncovered, at 450 degrees for 25 to 30 minutes or until tender, shaking pans and basting with orange juice mixture several times. Stir cilantro and remaining chili powder into sour cream; serve with warm fries. Makes 8 to 10 servings.

Tracy Zimmerman
Spirit Lake, IA

A yummy new partner
for hamburgers!

Herbed Cheese Focaccia ✓

13.8-oz. tube refrigerated
  <u>pizza dough</u>
1 onion, finely chopped
2 cloves garlic, minced
2 T. olive oil
1 t. dried basil
1 t. dried oregano
1/2 t. dried rosemary
1 c. shredded mozzarella cheese

Unroll dough on a greased baking
sheet. Press with fingers to form
indentations; set aside. Sauté onion
and garlic in oil in a skillet; remove
from heat. Stir in herbs; spread
mixture evenly over dough. Sprinkle
with cheese. Bake at 400 degrees for
10 to 15 minutes, until golden. Slice
into squares. Makes 12 to 14 servings.

51

Mary Ann Johnson
Sycamore, IL

Even tastier made with
fresh herbs! Substitute
one tablespoon of fresh
herbs for each teaspoon
of dried herbs.

Gingered Salmon Skewers

1 lb. boneless, skinless salmon
    fillet
10 to 12 wooden skewers, soaked
    in water
1/4 c. soy sauce
1/4 c. honey
1 T. rice wine vinegar or cider
    vinegar
1 t. fresh ginger, peeled and
    minced
1 clove garlic, minced
1/8 t. pepper
lemon wedges

Slice salmon lengthwise into 10 to
12 narrow strips. Thread each strip
onto a skewer; place skewers in a
shallow dish. Whisk together soy sauce,
honey, vinegar and spices. Pour over
skewers, turning to coat. Let stand at
room temperature for 30 minutes.
Drain marinade into a small saucepan;
simmer over medium-low heat for
several minutes. Grill skewers over
medium-high heat on a lightly oiled
grill, brushing often with marinade,
for 4 minutes on each side. Squeeze
lemon wedges over salmon; serve
warm. Makes 10 to 12 skewers.

Mary Lou Dell
Howell, MI

Slide grilled salmon strips
onto shredded lettuce for a
wonderful salad topping.

Spicy Honey-Molasses Wings ✓

5 lbs. chicken wings
2-1/2 c. spicy catsup
2/3 c. vinegar
1/2 c. plus 2 T. honey
1/2 c. molasses
1 t. salt
1 t. Worcestershire sauce
1/2 t. onion powder
1/2 t. chili powder
Optional: 1/2 to 1 t. smoke-
    flavored cooking sauce

Arrange wings in a greased
15"x10" jelly-roll pan. Bake,
uncovered, at 375 degrees for
30 minutes. Drain; turn wings
and return to oven for an additional
20 to 25 minutes. While wings are
baking, combine remaining
ingredients in a large saucepan.
Bring to a boil; reduce heat and
simmer, uncovered, for 25 to
30 minutes. Arrange one-third
of wings in a large slow cooker; top
with one cup sauce. Repeat layers
twice. Cover and cook on low setting
for 3 to 4 hours; stir gently before
serving. Makes about 4 dozen.

Dema Rankin
Gooseberry Patch

A party-pleaser...be
sure to have plenty of
paper napkins!

53

Party Perfect

Savory Bacon Bites

2 sweet onions, each sliced into
   8 wedges
8 thick slices hickory-smoked
   bacon, cut in half
8 6-inch wooden skewers,
   soaked in water
2 T. brown sugar, packed
2 T. balsamic vinegar
1 T. molasses

Wrap each onion wedge in a bacon slice. Arrange 2 wedges on each skewer; place in a shallow glass or plastic dish. Combine remaining ingredients; drizzle over skewers. Cover and refrigerate for one hour. Remove skewers from marinade, reserving marinade. Grill, covered, over medium-high heat for 20 minutes, or until onions are crisp-tender, occasionally turning and basting with reserved marinade. Makes 8 servings.

Jennifer Eveland-Kupp
Blandon, PA

We love to make these skewers every year as soon as sweet onions first arrive on produce stands.

Basil-Mushroom Pizza

2 T. butter
1 c. portabella mushrooms,
  sliced
2 cloves garlic, minced
12-inch Italian pizza crust
1 to 2 T. olive oil
1 c. spinach, sliced into
  1/2-inch strips
1/2 c. fresh basil, chopped
8-oz. pkg. shredded
  mozzarella cheese

Melt butter in a large skillet over medium heat. Add mushrooms and garlic; sauté just until tender, about 5 minutes. Place crust on an ungreased baking sheet; brush with oil. Sprinkle spinach evenly over crust, followed by basil, cheese and mushroom mixture. Bake at 350 degrees for 8 to 10 minutes, or until cheese is melted and edges of crust are crisp. Makes 4 servings.

Laurel Perry
Loganville, GA
You may just have to make more than one...they're that good!

Baja Bites

5 eggs, beaten
1 c. cottage cheese
1/4 c. all-purpose flour
1/2 t. baking powder ✗
1/4 c. butter, melted
2 T. green onion, minced
4-oz. can diced green chiles,
   drained
8-oz. pkg. shredded Monterey
   Jack cheese

Combine eggs and cottage cheese; mix
until almost smooth. Add flour, baking
powder and butter; stir in onion, chiles
and cheese. Pour into a lightly greased
8"x8" baking pan. Bake at 350 degrees
for 30 to 40 minutes. Cool slightly;
cut into squares. Makes 9 servings.

Pam Lewis
Munster, IN
Nice 'n spicy tidbits that
are oh-so easy to whip up!

Bruschetta with Cranberry Relish

1 French baguette loaf, sliced
    1/4-inch thick
1 to 2 T. olive oil
1 t. orange zest
1 t. lemon zest
1/2 c. chopped pecans
1/2 c. crumbled blue cheese

Brush baguette slices lightly with oil.
Arrange on a broiler pan; toast lightly
under broiler. Turn slices over;
spread with Cranberry Relish.
Sprinkle with zests, pecans and
blue cheese. Place under broiler
just until cheese begins to melt.
Makes 18 to 20 servings.

Cranberry Relish:

16-oz. can whole-berry
    cranberry sauce
6-oz. pkg. sweetened dried
    cranberries
1/2 c. sugar
1 t. rum extract
1 c. chopped pecans

Stir all ingredients together.

57

Rhonda Johnson
Studio City, CA

Serve these crisp, savory
slices at your next
Thanksgiving feast...
you may just start a
new tradition!

High Rollers

6 12-inch flour tortillas
2 8-oz. containers honey-nut
  cream cheese spread
3 c. baby spinach leaves
9-oz. pkg. deli oven-roasted
  turkey slices
6-oz. pkg. sweetened dried
  cranberries
Optional: seedless grapes

For each roll-up, spread a tortilla with 2 tablespoons cream cheese. Layer with spinach leaves; add 2 slices turkey to cover most of spinach. Spread another tablespoon cream cheese over turkey; sprinkle with one to 2 tablespoons cranberries. Roll up tightly; secure with a toothpick. Place tortilla rolls seam-side down on a tray; cover and chill for one to 2 hours. At serving time, trim off ends of rolls; slice 1/2-inch thick. Garnish with grapes, if desired. Makes about 5 dozen.

Michelle Sheridan
Gooseberry Patch

A new flavor twist on the familiar tortilla roll-ups we all love. Try honey-roasted turkey too... delightful!

Mini Ham & Swiss Cups

2-1/2 oz. pkg. deli ham,
   finely chopped
1 onion, finely chopped
1/2 c. shredded Swiss cheese
1 egg, beaten
1/2 t. Dijon mustard
1/8 t. pepper
8-oz. tube refrigerated
   crescent rolls

Combine ham and onion; add
cheese, egg, mustard and pepper.
Mix well and set aside. Unroll
crescent rolls; press dough into a
single large rectangle. Cut rectangle
into 24 squares; press each into a
lightly greased mini muffin cup. Fill
muffin cups with ham mixture. Bake
at 350 degrees for 13 to 15 minutes,
or until golden. Makes 2 dozen.

59

Shari Miller
Hobart, IN

Perfect for a shower,
brunch or lunch with your
best girlfriends! I'm
always being asked to
share this recipe.

Easy Potato Soup

4 to 5 potatoes, peeled and cubed
10-3/4 oz. can cream of
   celery soup
10-3/4 oz. can cream of
   chicken soup
1-1/4 c. water
4-2/3 c. milk
6.6-oz. pkg. instant potato flakes
Garnish: shredded Cheddar
   cheese, sliced green onions,
   crumbled bacon

Combine potatoes, soups and water in
a slow cooker. Cover and cook on high
setting until potatoes are tender, about
2 to 3 hours. Stir in milk; add potato
flakes to desired consistency, stirring
constantly. Cover and cook on high
setting an additional 2 to 3 hours
longer. Spoon into bowls to serve;
top with garnishes. Serves 4 to 6.

Jeanne West
Roanoke Rapids, NC
Serve piping-hot...is there
anything cozier on
a chilly day?

Beef Fajita Skewers

1 lb. boneless beef top sirloin,
   sliced into 1-inch cubes
8 wooden skewers, soaked
   in water
1 green pepper, cut into wedges
1 red or yellow pepper,
   cut into wedges
2 onions, cut into wedges
3 T. lime juice
1/3 c. Italian salad dressing
salt to taste

Thread beef cubes onto 4 skewers;
thread peppers and onions onto
remaining skewers. Combine lime
juice and salad dressing; brush
over skewers. Grill over hot coals
or on a medium-hot grill, turning
occasionally, 7 to 9 minutes for
beef and 12 to 15 minutes for
vegetables. Sprinkle with salt to
taste. Makes 8 servings.

61

Jerry Lyttle
St. Clair Shores, MI
Serve with warmed flour
tortillas, sour cream and
salsa...a clever new way
to enjoy a Mexican
restaurant favorite.

Sit Down & Enjoy
Italian Meatball Soup ✓

16-oz. pkg. frozen Italian-style
   meatballs
2 14-1/2 oz. cans beef broth
2 14-1/2 oz. cans diced tomatoes
   with Italian herbs
1 c. potato, peeled and diced
1/2 c. onion, chopped
1/4 t. garlic pepper
16-oz. pkg. frozen mixed
   vegetables

In a slow cooker, mix frozen meatballs, broth, tomatoes, potato, onion and garlic pepper. Cover and cook on low setting for 9 to 11 hours. Stir in frozen vegetables. Increase setting to high; cover and cook for one additional hour, or until vegetables are tender. Makes 4 to 6 servings.

Alice Hardin
Antioch, CA
Sprinkle with freshly shredded Parmesan cheese for added flavor.

Rosemary-Dijon Chicken Croissants

3 c. cooked chicken breast,
  chopped
1/3 c. green onion, chopped
1/4 c. smoked almonds, chopped
1/4 c. plain yogurt
1/4 c. mayonnaise
1 t. fresh rosemary, chopped
1 t. Dijon mustard
1/8 t. salt
1/8 t. pepper
10 mini croissants, split
Garnish: leaf lettuce

Combine all ingredients except
bread and lettuce, mixing well.
Arrange lettuce leaves inside
croissants; spread with chicken
mixture. Makes 10 mini sandwiches.

Jo Ann

Pair with fruit salad cups
and sweet tea for a
delightful brunch.

Grilled Roast Beef & Peppers

12-inch loaf Italian bread, halved
  lengthwise
1/2 lb. deli roast beef, sliced
1/4 lb. mozzarella cheese, sliced
8-oz. jar roasted red peppers,
  drained and chopped
2 T. green olives with pimentos,
  diced
1 T. olive oil

Layer bottom half of loaf with roast
beef, cheese, peppers and olives; add
top of loaf. Brush oil lightly over both
sides of loaf. Heat a large skillet over
medium heat; add loaf carefully and
cook for 2 to 3 minutes on each side,
until golden and cheese has melted.
Slice loaf into sections to serve. Makes
4 to 6 sandwiches.

Jennie Gist
Gooseberry Patch

A countertop grill works
well too...just place
the filled loaf inside,
close the lid and toast
until golden.

Chicken Ranch Quesadillas

1/2 c. ranch dip
8 8-inch flour tortillas
1 c. shredded Cheddar cheese
1 c. shredded Monterey Jack
  cheese
10-oz. can chicken, drained
1/3 c. bacon bits
Optional: salsa

Spread 2 tablespoons dip on each of 4 tortillas. Top each with one-quarter of the cheeses, chicken and bacon bits. Top with remaining tortillas. Place each tortilla stack in a lightly greased non-stick skillet or griddle over medium-high heat until lightly golden; turn carefully and cook until cheese is melted. Let stand for 2 minutes; slice into wedges. Serve with salsa, if desired. Serves 4.

65

Gretchen Brown
Forest Grove, OR

For an easy-to-handle party snack, slice each quesadilla into 8 mini wedges.

Divine Seafood Chowder

1 onion, sliced
4 potatoes, peeled and sliced
garlic to taste, minced
1 t. dill weed
2 T. butter
1 c. clam juice, heated to boiling
15-oz. can creamed corn
salt and pepper to taste
1/2 lb. haddock or cod fillet
1/2 lb. uncooked medium shrimp,
    peeled and halved
1 c. light cream, warmed

Layer all ingredients except cream in
a slow cooker, placing fish and shrimp
on top. Cover and cook on high setting
for one hour; reduce setting to low and
cook for 3 hours. Just before serving,
gently stir in cream. Makes 4 to
6 servings.

**Audrey Laudenat
East Haddam, CT**

This hearty chowder is
a meal all in itself!
Be sure to pass a basket
of oyster crackers.

Golden Crab Cakes

3 c. saltine crackers, crushed
   and divided
2 eggs, beaten
1/2 c. onion, diced
3 T. mayonnaise
1 T. mustard
2 t. lemon juice
1/2 t. salt
1/4 t. pepper
1/8 t. cayenne pepper
1/4 t. hot pepper sauce
1 lb. refrigerated fresh lump
   crabmeat
2 T. butter
2 T. oil
Garnish: tartar sauce

Stir together 2 cups cracker crumbs,
eggs, onion, mayonnaise, mustard,
lemon juice and seasonings. Fold in
crabmeat. Shape into eight, 3-inch
patties; dredge in remaining crumbs.
Melt butter and oil together in a
skillet over medium-high heat.
Cook crab cakes until golden, about
4 minutes on each side. Serve with
tartar sauce. Makes 8 servings.

Holly Higgins
Arnold, MD

Mix up some fresh tartar
sauce! Add a tablespoon
each of minced onion and
pickle relish to a cup of
mayonnaise and chill.

Cheesy Vegetable Soup

4 10-1/2 oz. cans chicken broth
2-1/2 c. potatoes, peeled
   and cubed
1 c. celery, chopped
1 c. onion, chopped
2-1/2 c. broccoli, chopped
2-1/2 c. cauliflower, chopped
2 10-3/4 oz. cans cream of
   chicken soup
16-oz. pkg. pasteurized process
   cheese spread, cubed
16-oz. pkg. pasteurized process
   Mexican cheese spread, cubed
1 lb. cooked ham, cubed

Combine broth, potatoes, celery and
onion in a large soup pot over medium
heat. Simmer until vegetables are
tender, about 20 minutes. Add broccoli
and cauliflower; simmer an additional
10 minutes. Stir in soup, cheeses and
ham; simmer until cheeses melt and
soup is heated through. Serves 8 to 10.

Belinda Gibson
Amarillo, TX

Oh my goodness...this is
the best soup I've ever
tasted! And it's so easy
to make too.

Giant Stuffed Sandwich

69

1/2 c. quick-cooking oats,
  uncooked
1/2 c. boiling water
2 T. butter
16-oz. pkg. hot roll mix
3/4 c. very warm water
  (110 to 115 degrees)
2 eggs, beaten
1/2 c. mayonnaise
1/4 c. coarse mustard
9-oz. pkg. sliced deli honey ham
6-oz. pkg. sliced deli roast turkey
6-oz. pkg. sliced deli roast
  chicken
1 to 2 tomatoes, thinly sliced
1 red onion, thinly sliced
8 slices Cheddar cheese
Garnish: shredded lettuce

Combine oats, boiling water and
butter in a large bowl; let stand for
5 minutes. Dissolve yeast from roll
mix in warm water; add to oat
mixture. Stir well; mix in eggs. Add
flour from roll mix; blend well. Form
into a 10-inch circle on a greased
12" pizza pan. Cover; let rise for
25 minutes, until double. Bake at
350 degrees for 25 minutes. Cool on
a wire rack; cut in half horizontally.
Whisk together mayo and mustard;
spread over cut sides. Assemble
sandwich and cut into wedges.
Serves 8 to 12.

Helen Williams
Heath, OH

No time to bake? Just pick
up a 12-inch round bread
loaf at the bakery to make
this picnic favorite.

Slow-Cooked Pulled Pork

1 T. oil
3-1/2 to 4-lb. boneless pork
   shoulder roast, tied
10-1/2 oz. can French onion soup
1 c. catsup
1/4 c. cider vinegar
2 T. brown sugar, packed
24 slices Texas toast or 12 sandwich
   rolls, split

Heat oil in a skillet over medium heat.
Add roast and brown on all sides;
remove to a large slow cooker and set
aside. Mix soup, catsup, vinegar and
brown sugar; pour over roast. Cover
and cook on low setting for 8 to
10 hours, until roast is fork-tender.
Remove roast to a platter; discard
string and let stand for 10 minutes.
Shred roast, using 2 forks; return
to slow cooker and stir. Spoon meat
and sauce onto bread slices or rolls.
Makes 12 sandwiches.

Tina Goodpasture
Meadowview, VA

A southern-style sandwich
favorite! Enjoy it like we
do, served with coleslaw
and dill pickles.

Buffalo Chicken Pizza

12-inch Italian pizza crust
1/4 c. butter, melted
1/4 c. hot pepper sauce
2 c. cooked chicken, diced
1/2 c. celery, chopped
4-oz. pkg. crumbled blue cheese

Place crust on a lightly greased
12" pizza pan; set aside. Combine
butter and pepper sauce; mix well.
Add chicken and celery, tossing to
coat. Spread chicken mixture evenly
over crust. Sprinkle with cheese.
Bake at 450 degrees for 10 to
12 minutes, or until heated through
and crust is crisp. Serves 4 to 6.

Kris Coburn
Dansville, NY

Hot pepper sauce is
available in several flavors
and heat levels...choose
one that's to your liking!

Tomato-Tortellini Soup

1 T. margarine
3 cloves garlic, minced
3 10-1/2 oz. cans chicken broth
8-oz. pkg. cheese-filled tortellini
1/4 c. grated Parmesan cheese
salt and pepper to taste
2/3 c. frozen chopped spinach,
    thawed and drained
14-1/2 oz. can Italian stewed
    tomatoes
1/2 c. tomato sauce

Melt margarine in a saucepan over
medium heat; add garlic. Sauté for
2 minutes; stir in broth and tortellini.
Bring to a boil; reduce heat. Mix in
Parmesan cheese, salt and pepper;
simmer until tortellini is tender. Stir
in spinach, tomatoes and tomato sauce;
simmer for 5 minutes, until heated
through. Serves 8 to 10.

Diane Bailey
Red Lion, PA

Mamma mia! This is oh-so
satisfying and really easy
to put together...ready in
about 20 minutes.

Fiesta Chicken Pronto

73

8 boneless, skinless chicken
   breasts
16-oz. can black beans,
   drained and rinsed
10-3/4 oz. can cream of
   chicken soup
2 T. taco seasoning mix
1/4 c. salsa
12 to 16 taco shells
Garnish: diced tomatoes, sliced
   jalapeño peppers, sliced olives

Arrange chicken in a slow cooker.
Combine remaining ingredients
except taco shells; pour over
chicken. Cover and cook on high
setting for 3 hours. Remove chicken;
shred and stir back into slow cooker.
Spoon into taco shells; garnish as
desired. Serves 8.

Kristi Duis
Maple Plain, NY
We like to serve this
spicy chicken in burritos...
mini tacos are fun for
parties too!

Ham & Pineapple Kabobs

2 lbs. smoked ham, cut into
   1-inch cubes
2 8-oz. cans pineapple chunks,
   drained and juice reserved
8 to 10 skewers, soaked in water
1/4 c. soy sauce
1/4 c. brown sugar, packed
1/4 t. ground ginger

Thread ham cubes and pineapple
chunks on skewers; place in an
ungreased 2-quart casserole dish.
Combine reserved juice and remaining
ingredients; pour over kabobs, turning
to coat. Cover and refrigerate for
2 hours, turning occasionally. Grill
over medium-hot coals, turning twice
and brushing with marinade until
hot and golden, about 10 minutes.
Makes 8 to 10 servings.

Stephanie Moon
Nampa, ID

Soak wooden kabob skewers
in water at least 20
minutes before using...they
won't burn or stick.

Easy Stromboli

1 loaf frozen bread dough,
    thawed
2 eggs, separated
2 T. oil
1 t. dried oregano
1 t. dried parsley
1/2 t. garlic powder
1/4 t. pepper
4-oz. pkg. sliced pepperoni
8-oz. pkg. shredded mozzarella
    cheese
1 T. grated Parmesan cheese

75

On a lightly floured surface, roll
out dough into a 15-inch by 12-inch
rectangle. Combine egg yolks, oil
and seasonings; spread over dough.
Arrange pepperoni and mozzarella
cheese over dough; sprinkle with
Parmesan cheese. Starting at one
long side, roll up; pinch ends to
seal. Place seam-side down on a
lightly greased baking sheet. Brush
with beaten egg whites. Bake at
350 degrees for 30 to 40 minutes,
until golden. Slice; serve warm.
Makes 8 servings.

Jane Evans
DeGraff, OH
Everyone loves stromboli!
I like to serve garlic
butter and warmed pizza
sauce on the side
for dipping.

Yummy Ham Sandwiches

6-lb. bone-in ham
8-oz. jar mustard
16-oz. pkg. brown sugar
24 dinner rolls, split

Place ham in a large slow cooker; cover with water. Cover and cook on low setting for 8 to 10 hours, until ham is very tender. Drain; let cool. Shred ham and return to slow cooker; stir in mustard and brown sugar. Cover and cook on low setting just until heated through. Serve on rolls. Makes 24 mini sandwiches.

Beth Cavanaugh
Westerville, OH

A nothing-to-it recipe that's always welcome at any carry-in dinner or potluck.

Beef Barley Soup

2 c. carrots, peeled and thinly
   sliced
1 c. celery, thinly sliced
3/4 c. red or green pepper, diced
1 c. onion, diced
1 lb. stew beef, cubed
1/2 c. pearl barley, uncooked
1/4 c. fresh parsley, chopped
3 cubes beef bouillon
2 T. catsup
1 t. salt
3/4 t. dried basil
5 c. water

Layer vegetables, beef and barley
in a slow cooker; add seasonings.
Pour water over all; do not stir.
Cover and cook on low setting
for 9 to 11 hours. Makes 4 to
6 servings.

Lynne McKaige
Savage, MN
For extra rich beef flavor,
use a heaping tablespoon of
powdered beef soup base in
place of the bouillon.

White Chicken Chili

2 onions, chopped
1 T. olive oil
6 c. chicken broth
6 15-1/2 oz. cans Great Northern
   beans, drained and rinsed
3 5-oz. cans chicken, drained
2 4-oz. cans diced green chiles
2 t. ground cumin
1 t. garlic powder
1-1/2 t. dried oregano
1/4 t. white pepper
12-oz. container sour cream
3 c. shredded Monterey
   Jack cheese

In a large stockpot over medium heat, sauté onions in oil until tender. Stir in remaining ingredients except sour cream and cheese. Simmer for 30 minutes, stirring frequently, until heated through. Shortly before serving time, add sour cream and cheese. Stir until cheese is melted. Serves 16 to 20.

Andrea Pocreva
San Antonio, TX
This chili recipe feeds a crowd! If you're hosting a smaller group, it is easily halved.

Tex-Mex Sloppy Joes

1-1/2 lbs. ground beef
1 c. onion, chopped
1 clove garlic, minced
3/4 c. spicy cocktail vegetable
    juice
3/4 c. catsup
1/2 c. water
2 T. brown sugar, packed
2 T. jalapeño peppers, chopped
1 T. mustard
2 t. chili powder
8 kaiser rolls, split and toasted
Garnish: Mexican-blend
    shredded cheese, sliced
    avocado, sliced jalapeño
    peppers, sliced black olives

In a skillet over medium heat, brown ground beef, onion and garlic; drain. Combine juice, catsup, water, brown sugar, peppers, mustard and chili powder in a slow cooker; stir in meat mixture. Cover and cook on low setting for 8 to 10 hours. Spoon meat mixture onto buns; garnish as desired. Makes 8 servings.

Anthony Fontana
Scottsdale, AZ
Wake up your taste buds
with this spicy version
of an old favorite.

French Onion Soup

1 T. butter
2 T. olive oil
4 onions, sliced
3 c. beef broth
3 to 4 bay leaves
salt and pepper to taste
6 slices French bread, toasted
3/4 c. shredded Swiss cheese

Heat butter and oil in a stockpot over medium heat until butter melts. Add onions; cook for 20 to 30 minutes, until dark golden. Add broth, bay leaves, salt and pepper. Bring to a boil; reduce heat, cover and simmer for 30 minutes. Discard bay leaves. Ladle soup into 6 oven-safe soup bowls; top each with a slice of bread and sprinkle with cheese. Set bowls on a sturdy baking sheet. Broil until cheese is melted and golden. Serves 6.

Barbara Feist Stienstra
Goshen, NY

The best French onion soup you'll ever eat! This recipe was created at the college where I worked for many years.

Sit Down & Enjoy

Incredible Mini Burger Bites

2 lbs. lean ground beef
1-1/2 oz. pkg. onion soup mix
2 eggs, beaten
1/2 c. dry bread crumbs
3 T. water
1/2 t. garlic salt
1 t. pepper
24 dinner rolls, split
6 slices American cheese,
   quartered
Garnish: catsup, mustard,
   shredded lettuce, thinly
   sliced onion, dill pickles

Mix first 7 ingredients in a bowl;
refrigerate for an hour. Spread
meat mixture over a greased large
baking sheet. Cover with plastic
wrap and roll out evenly with a rolling
pin. Discard plastic wrap; bake at
400 degrees for 12 minutes. Slice
into 24 squares with a pizza cutter.
Top each roll with a burger square,
a cheese slice and desired garnishes.
Makes 24 mini sandwiches.

Megan Besch
Omaha, NE

My family adores these...
yours will too! We make
them for football parties
and summer get-togethers.

Southwestern Pork Chalupas

2 15-oz. cans pinto beans, drained and rinsed
4 c. water
4-oz. can chopped green chiles
2 T. chili powder
2 t. ground cumin
1 t. dried oregano
salt and pepper to taste
4-lb. pork shoulder roast
16-oz. pkg. tortilla chips
Garnish: shredded Mexican-blend cheese, sour cream, salsa, sliced black olives, sliced jalapeño peppers

Combine beans, water, chiles and spices in a large slow cooker; mix well. Add roast; cover and cook on low setting for 4 hours. Remove roast and shred, discarding any bones; return pork to slow cooker. Cover and cook on low setting for an additional 2 to 4 hours, adding more water if necessary. To serve, arrange tortilla chips on serving plates. Spoon pork mixture over chips; garnish as desired. Makes 8 to 10 servings.

Vickie

Try these instead of ground beef nachos... family & friends will say Olé!

Chicken Pesto Pizza

2 boneless, skinless chicken
  breasts
1 T. olive oil
13.8-oz. tube refrigerated
  pizza dough
7-oz. jar basil pesto sauce
3 T. tomato sauce
14-1/2 oz. can petite diced
  tomatoes, drained
salt to taste
8-oz. pkg. shredded mozzarella
  cheese
2 T. Italian seasoning

83

In a skillet over medium heat,
brown chicken in oil. Remove to
cutting board to cool; chop finely
and set aside. Spread dough out
onto a greased baking sheet; pierce
surface of dough with a fork. Mix
together sauces and tomatoes; add
salt to taste. Stir in chicken; mix
well. Spread over dough; top with
cheese and Italian seasoning. Bake
at 400 degrees for 10 to 12 minutes,
until cheese is melted and bubbly.
Makes 6 to 8 servings.

Laura Witham
Anchorage, AK

When my husband and I
enjoyed a flavorful new
pizza at a local restaurant,
I just had to recreate it.

Sit Down & Enjoy
Grilled Shrimp

24 uncooked large shrimp,
   peeled and cleaned
1 onion, chopped
5 cloves garlic, diced
1/4 c. fresh parsley, chopped
8 leaves fresh basil, chopped
1 t. dry mustard
1 t. hot pepper sauce
1 t. salt
juice of 2 lemons
1/2 c. olive oil
1/2 t. seafood seasoning
4 to 6 wooden skewers, soaked
   in water

Place shrimp in a large plastic zipping
bag. Mix remaining ingredients
together; pour over shrimp. Seal bag
and refrigerate for 24 hours, turning
bag several times to coat shrimp with
marinade. Drain and discard marinade;
place 4 to 6 shrimp on each skewer.
Place on a medium-high grill over hot
coals. Grill for 4 to 8 minutes until
slightly brownish pink; do not overcook.
Serve warm. Makes 4 to 6 servings.

Wendy Lee Paffenroth
Pine Island, NY

Grill some crusty garlic
bread alongside the shrimp,
for a meal that's perfect
on a lazy summer day!

Rio Grande Green Pork Chili

3 lbs. boneless pork steak, cubed
1 clove garlic, minced
3 T. olive oil
1/2 c. all-purpose flour
2 14-1/2 oz. cans beef broth
32-oz. can tomato juice
14-1/2 oz. can crushed tomatoes
7-oz. can diced green chiles
4-oz. can chopped jalapeño
    peppers
1/3 c. dried parsley
1/4 c. lemon juice
2 t. ground cumin
1 t. sugar
1/4 t. ground cloves

In a heavy skillet over medium heat, sauté pork and garlic in oil. Add flour, stirring until thoroughly mixed. Drain; transfer browned pork to a slow cooker. Add remaining ingredients. Cover and cook on low setting for 6 to 8 hours, until pork is tender. Serves 12 to 14.

Debby Heatwole
Canadian, TX
Serve generous bowls of this hearty stew, accompanied by tortilla chips and shredded cheese, for a savory buffet dish.

Crunchy Fish Nuggets with Dill Sauce

Stella Hickman
Gooseberry Patch

Buttermilk and cornmeal give these nuggets an old-fashioned taste kids and grown-ups will love.

1 egg, beaten
2 c. buttermilk
3 c. cornmeal
salt and pepper to taste
Optional: lemon pepper or
    cayenne pepper to taste
2 lbs. catfish, cod or haddock
    fillets, cut into 1-inch cubes
oil for deep frying

In a shallow bowl, whisk together egg and buttermilk. Place cornmeal in a separate bowl; add salt, pepper and other seasoning, as desired. Dip fish into egg mixture, then into cornmeal to coat. Pour several inches of oil into a deep fryer; heat to 375 degrees. Add fish to oil, a few pieces at a time. Cook for 2 to 3 minutes on each side, until golden and fish flakes easily with a fork. Drain on paper towels. Serve hot with Dill Sauce. Makes 6 to 8 servings.

Dill Sauce:

1/2 c. mayonnaise
1/2 c. sour cream or plain yogurt
2 t. dill weed
pepper to taste

Combine all ingredients. Serve immediately or keep chilled.

Mushroom Meatballs

2 10-3/4 oz. cans cream of
  mushroom soup
1-1/2 oz. pkg. onion soup mix
1 onion, chopped
2-lb. pkg. frozen meatballs,
  thawed
Optional: fresh parsley or green
  onion, chopped

Mix together soup, soup mix and
onion in a slow cooker. Add
meatballs and stir to coat. Cover and
cook on high setting for 2 hours.
Reduce heat to low setting; cook
an additional 2 to 4 hours. Garnish
as desired. Serves 6 to 8.

87

Shirley Moench
Garfield, MN

A terrific appetizer...or
stir in some cream to make
more gravy and serve over
buttered egg noodles. Yum!

Apple Cider Punch ✓

6 c. apple cider
2 c. cranberry-raspberry
   juice cocktail
1/2 c. lemon juice
25.4-oz. bottle sparkling white
   grape juice
Optional: 1 apple, thinly sliced

Combine cider, cranberry-raspberry juice and lemon juice in a large pitcher or punch bowl. Slowly add sparkling juice; serve immediately. If desired, garnish glasses with apple slices. Makes 15 servings.

Rosie Jones
Wabash, IN

For toasting a festive occasion, replace the grape juice with sparkling white wine.

Almond Toffee Popcorn

12 c. popped popcorn
1 c. sugar
1/2 c. butter
1/2 c. light corn syrup
1/4 c. water
1 c. chopped almonds, toasted
1/2 t. vanilla extract

Place popcorn in a large heat-proof bowl; remove any unpopped kernels and set aside. In a large saucepan, combine remaining ingredients except vanilla. Cook over medium-high heat, stirring occasionally, until mixture reaches the soft-crack stage, or 270 to 289 degrees on a candy thermometer. Remove from heat; add vanilla and stir well. Pour over popcorn, mixing until coated. Spread on wax paper to dry. Makes about 12 cups.

89

Erin Jones
Smyer, TX

Movie night will be extra special with a big bowl of this crunchy, nutty popcorn for snacking!

Island Fruit Salsa & Cinnamon Crisps

Angela Perry
Versailles, KY

Fresh fruit and veggies
mingle happily in this
dippable delight! It's a
scrumptious topping for
grilled fish too.

1 c. pineapple, peeled and diced
1 c. mango, peeled and diced
2/3 c. kiwi fruit, peeled and diced
1/2 c. yellow pepper, diced
1/2 c. red pepper, diced
1/2 c. red onion, finely chopped
1/4 c. fresh cilantro, chopped
1 t. lime juice
salt and pepper to taste

Combine all ingredients in a serving
bowl. Chill for one hour to allow flavors
to blend. Makes about 4-1/2 cups.

Cinnamon Crisps:

1/2 t. vanilla extract
1 T. hot water
1/2 t. cinnamon
3 T. sugar
4 6-inch flour tortillas, each cut
    into 8 wedges

Combine vanilla and water in a cup;
blend cinnamon and sugar in a separate
cup. Brush vanilla mixture over both
sides of tortilla wedges; sprinkle with
cinnamon-sugar. Place on a baking
sheet sprayed with non-stick vegetable
spray. Bake at 450 degrees for
5 minutes, until crisp. Makes about
2-1/2 dozen.

Summertime Iced Tea

4 c. boiling water
2 family-size teabags
6 leaves fresh mint
6-oz. can frozen lemonade
   concentrate
1 c. sugar
5 c. cold water
Garnish: ice cubes, fresh
   mint sprigs

Pour boiling water into a large
heatproof pitcher. Add teabags and
mint leaves; let stand for 5 minutes.
Discard teabags and mint leaves.
Add frozen lemonade, sugar and
cold water, mixing well. Serve over
ice; garnish with mint sprigs. Makes
about 10 servings.

Charlotte Harding
Starkville, MS
Freeze sprigs of fresh
mint in ice cubes for a
party-pretty touch.

Maple Hot Chocolate ✓

1/4 c. sugar
1 T. baking cocoa
1/8 t. salt
1/4 c. hot water
1 T. butter
4 c. milk
1 t. maple flavoring
1 t. vanilla extract
12 marshmallows, divided

Combine sugar, cocoa and salt in a large saucepan. Stir in hot water and butter; bring to a boil over medium heat. Add milk, maple flavoring, vanilla and 8 marshmallows. Heat through, stirring occasionally, until marshmallows are melted. Ladle into 4 mugs; top with remaining marshmallows. Makes 4 servings.

Debi DeVore
Dover, OH

Chocolatey made-from-scratch hot cocoa...even yummier with a little maple flavoring stirred in!

Warm Apple Cake

Doris Dell
Youngwood, PA

Warm out of the oven, drizzled with homemade caramel sauce...very comforting with a cup of spiced tea.

1 c. all-purpose flour
1 c. sugar
1 t. baking soda
1 t. cinnamon
1/4 t. salt
1 egg, beaten
2 c. apples, cored, peeled and grated
1/2 c. chopped walnuts, divided

Combine first 5 ingredients in a large bowl. Mix together egg, apples and 1/4 cup nuts; add to flour mixture. Spread in a greased 8"x8" baking pan. Bake at 350 degrees for 25 to 30 minutes, until a toothpick tests clean. Serve warm, topped with Caramel Sauce and remaining nuts. Serves 9.

Caramel Sauce:

1/2 c. brown sugar, packed
2 T. all-purpose flour
1/8 t. salt
1 c. water
1 T. butter
1/4 t. vanilla extract

Combine sugar, flour and salt in a saucepan over medium heat; gradually stir in water. Cook and stir to a boil; cook for one to 2 minutes, until thickened. Remove from heat; stir in butter and vanilla.

93

Rosemary Lemon-Pineapple Punch

46-oz. can unsweetened
   pineapple juice
1-1/2 c. lemon juice
2 c. water
3/4 to 1 c. sugar, divided
4 to 5 sprigs fresh rosemary
1-ltr. bottle ginger ale, chilled

In a large saucepan, combine pineapple juice, lemon juice, water, 3/4 cup sugar and rosemary sprigs. Bring to a boil over medium heat, stirring until sugar dissolves. Remove from heat; cover and let stand for 15 minutes. Discard rosemary; chill. At serving time, add ginger ale; serve immediately. Makes 12 servings.

Helene Hamilton
Hickory, NC

So refreshing...just right for a garden party or reception.

Tropical Treat Bars ✓

1-1/2 c. graham cracker crumbs
1/2 c. butter, melted
14-oz. can sweetened
   condensed milk
1 c. sweetened dried pineapple,
   coarsely chopped
1 c. white chocolate chips
1-1/3 c. sweetened flaked coconut
1 c. macadamia nuts or almonds,
   coarsely chopped

Mix together graham cracker crumbs and melted butter. Press firmly into the bottom of an ungreased 13"x9" baking pan. Pour condensed milk evenly over crumb mixture. Sprinkle with pineapple, chocolate chips, coconut and nuts, pressing down firmly. Bake at 350 degrees for 25 to 30 minutes, until golden. Cool completely, chilling if desired. Cut into bars. Makes 2 dozen.

95

**Ruby Hempy
Largo, FL**

Cut into oversize bars...
cookie lovers will
be grateful!

Cappuccino Cooler ✓

1-1/2 c. brewed coffee, cooled
1-1/2 c. chocolate ice cream,
    softened
1/4 c. chocolate syrup
crushed ice
Garnish: frozen whipped topping,
    thawed
Optional: chocolate-covered
    espresso beans

Blend coffee, ice cream and syrup together until smooth; set aside. Fill 4 glasses 3/4 full with crushed ice; pour in coffee mixture. Top each with a dollop of whipped topping and an espresso bean, if desired. Serve immediately. Makes 4 servings.

Dianne Gregory
Sheridan, AR

A perfect pick-me-up beverage to share with your girlfriends after a day of antiquing or flea marketing.

Black Bottom Cupcakes

2 8-oz. pkgs. <u>cream cheese</u>,
  softened
2 eggs, beaten
2-2/3 c. sugar, divided
1-1/4 t. salt, divided
1-1/2 c. semi-sweet chocolate chips
3 c. all-purpose flour
2 t. baking soda
1/2 c. baking cocoa
2 c. water
2/3 c. oil
2 T. <u>white vinegar</u>
2 t. vanilla extract

Combine cream cheese, eggs, 2/3 cup sugar, 1/4 teaspoon salt and chocolate chips; mix well. In a separate bowl, combine remaining ingredients; beat well. Fill paper-lined muffin cups 2/3 full; top each with a heaping teaspoon of cheese mixture. Bake at 350 degrees for 25 to 30 minutes. Let cool; frost. Makes 2 to 3 dozen.

Buttercream Frosting:

1 c. butter, softened
6 T. milk
6 c. powdered sugar, divided
2 t. vanilla extract

Blend butter, milk and 2 cups sugar well; add remaining sugar and vanilla. Beat with an electric mixer on medium-high until fluffy.

Gretchen Brown
Forest Grove, OR

A dear friend gave me this wonderful recipe years ago as a wedding shower gift.

Strawberry-Watermelon Slush

1 pt. strawberries, hulled and
  halved
2 c. watermelon, seeded and cubed
1/3 c. sugar
1/3 c. lemon juice
2 c. ice cubes

Combine strawberries, watermelon,
sugar and lemon juice in a blender.
Blend until smooth. Gradually add
ice and continue to blend. Serve
immediately. Makes 5 to 6 servings.

Sandy Benham
Sanborn, NY

A luscious combination
of fresh summer fruit.
Slip a plump strawberry
onto a drinking straw
for a fun garnish.

Vickie's Chocolate Fondue

24-oz. pkg. semi-sweet chocolate
 chips
1 pt. whipping cream
6 T. light corn syrup
2 T. orange extract
cake cubes, fruit for dipping

Place chocolate chips in the top of a
double boiler. Melt over simmering
water; stir until smooth. Add
remaining ingredients and stir to
blend. Spoon into a fondue pot
or mini slow cooker on low setting
to keep warm. Serve with cake cubes
and fruit for dipping. Makes about
2-1/2 cups.

99

Vickie
Delicious dipping for
squares of pound cake,
fresh pineapple cubes,
marshmallows...even graham
cracker sticks and pretzels!

Fresh Fruit Kabobs & Poppy Seed Dip

6 c. fresh fruit like strawberries, kiwi, pineapple, honeydew and cantaloupe, peeled and cut into bite-size cubes or slices
8 to 10 wooden skewers

Arrange fruit pieces alternately on skewers. Serve dip alongside fruit kabobs. Makes 8 to 10 servings.

Poppy Seed Dip:

1 c. vanilla yogurt
2 T. honey
4 t. lime juice
1 t. vanilla extract
1 t. poppy seed

Stir together ingredients in a small bowl. Keep chilled.

Anita Williams
Pikeville, KY

Try grilling these kabobs for a new spin. Place skewers over medium-high heat for 3 to 5 minutes... yum!

Chocolotta Pizza

Rebecca Mosher
Crosset, AR

I got this recipe from a good friend of mine and made a few additions so it's even richer. Great for kids' sleepovers!

12-oz. pkg. semi-sweet chocolate chips
8 2-oz. sqs. white melting chocolate, divided
2 c. mini marshmallows
1 c. crispy rice cereal
6-oz. jar maraschino cherries, drained and halved
16-oz. pkg. chocolate-covered peanuts
1 t. oil

101

Combine chocolate chips and 7 squares white chocolate in a 2-quart microwave-safe bowl. Microwave on high setting for 2 minutes; stir. Microwave an additional one to 2 minutes until smooth, stirring every 30 seconds. Stir in marshmallows and cereal. Spoon onto a greased 12" pizza pan. Top with cherries and peanuts, pressing gently. Microwave remaining white chocolate with oil for one minute; stir. Microwave for 30 seconds to one minute, until smooth, stirring every 15 seconds. Drizzle over pizza; chill until firm. Keep refrigerated. Let stand at room temperature for 10 to 15 minutes before slicing into wedges. Makes 10 to 12 servings.

Mini Ice Cream Sundaes

Sharon Striker
Dallas, OR

Fun sized! Use one-ounce
mini tumblers...guests
can try one or sample
'em all! Dollop with
whipped topping.

Black Forest Sundaes:

12 chocolate sandwich cookies, crushed
1 pt. vanilla ice cream
21-oz. can cherry pie filling
12-oz. jar hot fudge topping
1/2 c. chopped walnuts

Divide ingredients among sundae cups,
layering in order given.

Bananas Foster Sundaes:

2 to 3 ripe bananas, sliced
2 T. butter
1 c. brown sugar, packed
1 t. vanilla extract
1/2 t. cinnamon
1/8 t. salt
1 pt. butter pecan ice cream

Sauté bananas in butter for 2 minutes.
Add sugar, vanilla, cinnamon and salt;
cook and stir for 2 minutes, until
thickened. Cool slightly. Divide ice
cream among sundae cups. Spoon
topping over ice cream.

Key West Sundaes:

16 whole graham crackers, crushed
1/4 c. butter, melted
1 T. sugar
1 pt. lime sherbet
Garnish: lime wedges

Toss together crackers, butter and sugar;
press into a 9"x9" baking pan. Bake at
350 degrees for 8 to 10 minutes, until
golden. Cool; crumble coarsely. Layer
crumb mixture with sherbet in sundae
cups; garnish.

Classic Raisin Oatmeal Cookies

3/4 c. butter
1 c. brown sugar, packed
1/2 c. sugar
1/4 c. milk
1 egg
1 t. vanilla extract
1 c. all-purpose flour
1 t. cinnamon
1/2 t. baking soda
1/4 t. salt
3 c. long-cooking oats,
   uncooked
1 c. chopped walnuts
1 c. raisins

Combine butter, sugars, milk, egg
and vanilla in a large bowl. Beat until
light and fluffy; set aside. Whisk
together flour, cinnamon, baking
soda and salt. Add to butter mixture;
stir well. Add oats, walnuts and
raisins. Drop by teaspoonfuls
onto greased baking sheets. Bake
in upper third of oven at 350 degrees
for 12 to 15 minutes. Makes 3 dozen.

103

Helen Gaulke
Newark, OH

Real old-fashioned
cookie-jar cookies! Serve
with big glasses
of icy milk.

Fresh-Squeezed Lemonade

1-3/4 c. sugar
8 c. cold water, divided
6 to 8 lemons
Garnish: ice cubes, lemon slices

Combine sugar and one cup water in a small saucepan. Bring to a boil; stir until sugar dissolves. Cool to room temperature; chill. Juice lemons to measure 1-1/2 cups juice; remove seeds and strain pulp, if desired. In a large pitcher, stir together chilled syrup, juice and remaining water. Chill for several hours to blend flavors. Serve over ice cubes; garnish with lemon slices. Makes 8 to 10 servings.

Pat Sharrot
Circleville, OH

There's nothing like homemade lemonade on a hot day...and it's really so easy to make.

pizza dough — focaccia p. 51
— grk pizza p 43

Butterscotch Cheesecake Bars

6-oz. pkg. butterscotch chips
1/3 c. butter
2 c. graham cracker crumbs
1 c. chopped pecans
8-oz. pkg. cream cheese, softened
14-oz. can sweetened condensed milk
1 t. vanilla extract
1 egg, beaten

105

Melt butterscotch chips and butter in a saucepan over medium-low heat; stir in cracker crumbs and pecans. Press half of mixture into an ungreased 13"x9" baking pan. Beat cream cheese in a large bowl until fluffy; stir in condensed milk. Add vanilla and egg; mix well and pour over crumb mixture. Top with remaining crumb mixture. Bake at 350 degrees for 25 to 30 minutes. Chill until firm; cut into bars. Makes about 1-1/2 dozen.

Marsha Konken
Sterling, CO

A bake-sale favorite!
Cut into small squares
and set each in a frilled
cupcake paper for
a pretty presentation.

Caramel-Coffee Tassies

Staci Meyers
Cocoa, FL

Bite-size tarts with a buttery caramel filling... delectable!

3-oz. pkg. cream cheese, softened
1/2 c. butter, softened
1 c. all-purpose flour
14-oz. pkg. caramels, unwrapped
1/4 c. evaporated milk
1-1/2 t. coffee liqueur or brewed
   coffee

Beat cream cheese and butter together until well blended; stir in flour. Form into a ball; chill for one hour to overnight. Shape into 1/2-inch balls; press each into an ungreased mini muffin cup. Bake at 350 degrees for 10 to 15 minutes, until golden. Let cool. Combine caramels and milk in a saucepan over medium heat; stir frequently until melted. Remove from heat; stir in liqueur or coffee. Spoon filling into baked shells; let cool. Pipe on frosting. Makes 2 dozen.

Mocha Frosting:

1 c. shortening
2/3 c. sugar
2/3 c. evaporated milk, chilled
1 t. coffee liqueur or brewed coffee

Blend shortening and sugar well; add evaporated milk and liqueur or coffee. Beat with an electric mixer on medium-high until fluffy, about 7 to 10 minutes.

Hot Mulled Cider

1 qt. water
4-inch cinnamon stick
2 t. allspice
1/8 t. ground cloves
1 gal. apple cider
12-oz. can frozen lemonade
   concentrate
juice of 2 oranges
1/3 c. honey
1 teabag

Combine water and spices in a large saucepan. Bring to a boil; reduce heat and simmer gently for 20 minutes. Combine remaining ingredients in a large pitcher; mix well and add to saucepan. Simmer until hot; discard cinnamon stick and teabag. Makes 18 to 20 servings.

107

Glenna Tooman
Boise, ID

Headed for a hometown parade? Tote along a thermos of this hot, spicy cider!

INDEX

INDEX

How did Gooseberry Patch get started?

Gooseberry Patch started in 1984 one day over the backyard fence in Delaware, Ohio. We were next-door neighbors who shared a love of collecting antiques, gardening and country decorating. Though neither of us had any experience (Jo Ann was a first-grade school teacher and Vickie, a flight attendant & legal secretary), we decided to try our hands at the mail-order business. Since we both had young children, this was perfect for us. We could work from our kitchen tables and keep an eye on the kids too! As our children grew, so did our "little" business. We moved into our own building in the country and filled the shelves to the brim with kitchenware, quilts, gourmet goodies, enamelware, mixing bowls and our very own line of cookbooks, calendars and organizers. We're so glad you're a part of our **Gooseberry Patch** family!

Vickie & Jo Ann

Call for a FREE catalog
of country delights

1·800·854·6673

Visit our website anytime: **www.gooseberrypatch.com**

U.S. to Canadian Recipe Equivalents

Volume Measurements

1/4 teaspoon	1 mL
1/2 teaspoon	2 mL
1 teaspoon	5 mL
1 tablespoon = 3 teaspoons	15 mL
2 tablespoons = 1 fluid ounce	30 mL
1/4 cup	60 mL
1/3 cup	75 mL
1/2 cup = 4 fluid ounces	125 mL
1 cup = 8 fluid ounces	250 mL
2 cups = 1 pint = 16 fluid ounces	500 mL
4 cups = 1 quart	1 L

Weights

1 ounce	30 g
4 ounces	120 g
8 ounces	225 g
16 ounces = 1 pound	450 g

Oven Temperatures

300° F	150° C
325° F	160° C
350° F	180° C
375° F	190° C
400° F	200° C
450° F	230° C

Baking Pan Sizes

Square

8x8x2 inches	2 L = 20x20x5 cm
9x9x2 inches	2.5 L = 23x23x5 cm

Rectangular

13x9x2 inches	3.5 L = 33x23x5 cm

Loaf

9x5x3 inches	2 L = 23x13x7 cm

Round

8x1-1/2 inches	1.2 L = 20x4 cm
9x1-1/2 inches	1.5 L = 23x4 cm

Recipe Abbreviations

t. = teaspoon	ltr. = liter
T. = tablespoon	oz. = ounce
c. = cup	lb. = pound
pt. = pint	doz. = dozen
qt. = quart	pkg. = package
gal. = gallon	env. = envelope

Kitchen Measurements

A pinch = 1/8 tablespoon	1 fluid ounce = 2 tablespoons
3 teaspoons = 1 tablespoon	4 fluid ounces = 1/2 cup
2 tablespoons = 1/8 cup	8 fluid ounces = 1 cup
4 tablespoons = 1/4 cup	16 fluid ounces = 1 pint
8 tablespoons = 1/2 cup	32 fluid ounces = 1 quart
16 tablespoons = 1 cup	16 ounces net weight = 1 pound
2 cups = 1 pint	
4 cups = 1 quart	
4 quarts = 1 gallon	